Chasing Wild Grief

Chasing Wild Grief

Poems by

Sandra J. Lindow

© 2021 Sandra J. Lindow. All rights reserved.
This material may not be reproduced in any form, published,
reprinted, recorded, performed, broadcast,
rewritten or redistributed without
the explicit permission of Sandra J. Lindow.
All such actions are strictly prohibited by law.

Cover design by Shay Culligan

ISBN: 978-1-63980-029-2

Kelsay Books
502 South 1040 East, A-119
American Fork, Utah 84003
Kelsaybooks.com

For Michael

4/15/1950
To
4/4/2017

Acknowledgments

Ariel Anthology, 2018: "After Mary Oliver's 'Wild Geese': Grieving Reconsidered"
Ariel Anthology, 2019: "On Walking to Water"
Ariel Anthology, 2020: "Discovery"
A Walk with Nature: "Cemetery Walk"
Asimov's, 2020: "Darning"
Barstow and Grand, 2018: "Niagara or Nothing"
Blue Heron, 2021: "In late September I plant Dutch Iris bulbs,"
Climbing Lightly through Forests: A Poetry Anthology Honoring Ursula K. Le Guin, Aqueduct, 2021: "The Scent of Green"
Free Verse, 2008: "Lambing Time"
Free Verse, 2009: "Feeding the Birds"
haikuniverse, 2020: "walking in March"
Nourish, 2018: "Powers"
Parentheses Journal: "Waltzing with Widow's Tears"
Portage Magazine, 2021: "April 15"
Red Cedar, 2018: "A Corona of Women"
Red Cedar, 2019: "The Great Unknowing," "Winged Grief"
Red Cedar, 2021: "In September I plant Dutch Iris bulbs"
Rosebud, 2018: "Junction Trail Revisited"
Shorts Magazine: "Tundra Swans"
Sky Island Journal, 2018: "Negative Space"
Twig, 2018: "February Flurry"
2020 Wisconsin Poets' Calendar: "One Year, One Month"
2021 Wisconsin Poets' Calendar: "Mind Music"
2022 Wisconsin Poets' Calendar: "Glissando for Wordsworth"

"All Along Junction Trail," 2020 Muse Prize Winner
"The Romance of Dragonflies," 2017 Triad 2nd Prize Winner
"Darning," 2021 SFPA Rhysling 3rd Prize Winner

I would like to thank the editors who published these poems, especially Michael Kriesel for his encouragement to publish this book; Max Garland, Karla Huston, Marilyn Taylor, and Laurel Winter for their thoughtful endorsements; Jennifer Grant for her cover photo; F.J. Bergmann for the author photo, the Women in Good Company for reminding me that I do not walk alone, my writing group for their thoughtful critiques, and all my friends and family for loving me during this difficult time.

Contents

Red Cedar Spring, May 2021   13

PreAmbles

Lambing Time   17
Feeding the Birds   18
September Sunday Road Trip   19
Cemetery Walk   20

Chasing Wild Grief

Powers   25
Niagara, or Nothing, February 2017   26
Haibun for Evergreen Cemetery in Winter   27
Mad as a March Hare: March 2, 2017   28
your death   29
The Romance of Dragonflies*   30
Waltzing with Widow's Tears   31
After You   32
Corona of Women   33
The Great Unknowing   34
After Mary Oliver's "Wild Geese": Grieving
    Reconsidered*   35
Twiggy   36
Negative Space   37
Winged Grief   38
Tree Trimming   39
February Flurry   40
One Year, One Month   41
Walking with Turtles   42
The Scent of Green   43
Chasing Wild Grief   44
Squirrel's Eye View   45

Junction Trail Revisited

Junction Trail Revisited	49
Darning	50
Walking in March	51
April 15	52
Glissando for Wordsworth	53
For Michael: All Along Junction Trail	54
South of the lake	56
On Walking to Water:	57
Mind Music	58
In late September I plant Dutch Iris bulbs,	59
March, Cirque du Soul	60
Tundra Swans	61
Discovery	62
October, Junction Trail Redux	63

Red Cedar Spring, May 2021

Through greening riverbank brush,
a great blue heron stands dreaming,
watching the Red Cedar body breaking

and sparkling over rocks, a good
place to fish but not fishing, perhaps
finding too much pleasure in the sun,

and that unity where broken water
becomes light: As the Japanese art
of kintsugi binds porcelain shards

with molten gold, brokenness
becomes ascendance, miming
how nature binds every broken thing.

As dandelions ascend a brush pile
of broken bridal wreath, the heron's
wild light ascends a broken heart.

PreAmbles

Lambing Time

Year twenty-five of our marriage,
blue sky, cold-footed robins, crows
in the corn stubble, gray slips of dying snow.
Planting will be late this year.
March wind blows us to a farm
to see newborn lambs.
We go alone; our children are grown.

If you love me, feed my sheep.

Distance widens between us as I walk ahead
toward a red-sided barn happy with children
feeding lambs and holding chicks.
Inside, you, just recovering from an illness,
stand transfixed by lambs, each spray-painted
with the same number as its browsy, patient mother.

"Come," I say impatient, "See the llamas."
Down the aisle, two llamas, mother and son
have captured attention. A sign names
the youngster's exotic eyes
—one brown, one blue—*watch eyes.*

Your eyes are brown, mine blue.
Together, our watch eyes measure
the unspoken distance between us.
Turning, we touch hands for a moment.
Our children are grown.
Planting will be late this year.

If you love me, feed my sheep.

Feeding the Birds

Against a dismal gray December sky, sparrows, nuthatches
    and cardinals share seeds on our balcony feeder.
    More polite than students in a crowded beer bar,
    they wait their turn, glide in, take a seed, then go,
    no interspecies squabbling or hogging. Perhaps
    that's seen as too mammalian although I've known
    a selfish swan or two for whom theirs was theirs,
    and mine was theirs, too.

A hairy woodpecker arrives, red head bouncing like a balloon,
    flag to my memory—the raucous pigeons I fed
    in Trafalgar Square, hail-fellows-well-met in uproarious
    to-do around my head and shoulders until the corn
    was gone from my cup; the elderly gentleman on a
    bench in Paris, sitting so still, feeding sparrows who
    patiently lined his arms.

Who are we to feed the birds?
    Is it that we seek sympathetic magic, yearning
    for flight on Icarian wings, that nearly effortless
    thwarting of gravity? "Look," you say, "An eagle!"
    Darkness boomerangs in from the hills, fierce and
    compassionless as an Old Testament god, settles like
    early winter atop a tree in a neighbor's yard, sits
    nearly motionless, scanning the horizon,
    unsettling this peaceable kingdom.

Who are we to feed the birds?

September Sunday Road Trip

The early frost predicted by the cool summer has not occurred.
We drive to an Alpaca Farm, late September clouds rumpling
the horizon like the pillows and sheets we left behind.

Autumn surrounds us: asters and golden rod decorating ditches,
small birds unzipping the high lines, a reprieve
of unharvested corn heavy in the fields.

Dry leaves skitter, jitterbug the pavement like cartoon animals.
Directions are clear. We arrive to find an amazement
of multi-colored alpaca, no Herefords or Holsteins here.

Inside the barn, craftswomen explain shearing, carding
and spinning, demonstrate the making of felt hats
while black, brown, dappled, and white alpaca wander

in small, convivial groups—friends at a lawn party—silent
but for the slippery soft accompaniment
of toothless upper jaws scraping meadow grass.

Like some long-married couples, a kind of wordless
telepathy seems to guide them outward toward novelty,
then homeward to nest. Midway across the meadow,

a newborn infant wears a brilliant blue jacket, wobbles
its first knock-kneed steps to suck. Light shifts,
clouds clear, and suddenly it feels like spring.

Cemetery Walk

Early April rain beads waterproof jackets; as we walk past
    Butch's Bay, a strange cloud rises three feet above
        slushy backwater ice, dissipates to mizzle.

Though icy water shivers the shoreline, a crew of die-hard ice
    fishers hunch on stools, looking from a distance like half-
        drunk, backwards question marks staring into holes.

"Who would want to do that?" we ask,
    with that certain smugness
        of long shared opinion.

We cross the land bridge and up stone steps into Evergreen
    Cemetery where the dazzled dust of centuries rests
        among temporarily soddened stones.

Boot soles squish, along muddy pale green ribbons, winding
    between rows of old and new markers, suffering
        and attachment, tangible above these final homes.

Here a good woman who was once my mother-in-law,
    up ahead, a sleeping lamb spans the fleet days of a three-
        year-old boy who died a hundred years ago.

Around the curve, an ornate concrete tree trunk
    celebrates the abbreviated life
        of "Our Beloved Lena."

What is it we carve in each other, as decades slide silently past,
    the slip of almost unfelt knives
        shaping our stony epitaphs?

Memory's amorphous mist answers, rises from the lake
 where it was cast, separate stories coming together,
  moving away each step we take.

Black birds line tree limbs, stalwart, rain-coated spectators of our
 meager parade. "Why do you do that?" I ask a fisherman.
  "Hey," he says, "It's a beautiful day."

Chasing Wild Grief

Powers

*Danger. Due to ... operation of the generator ...
the water ... may at any time change quickly
from low ... quiet to high ... turbulent.
There will be no warning.* *

January dazzles thaw; whirlpools roil
from the sluice below Red Cedar Dam,
where hydraulic rapids pulse, saucer
outward while crisscrossing power lines
diverge uphill as trail follows riverbank
and winds under the timber trestle bridge.

Below, sun dogs the river, white water
ripping around the rocky manmade island,
old snow shrugging to the ragged shoreline
where one tree bent horizontal still bears
a sun-struck ballet of flirting ice fans.
Above, an eagle cleaves a piece of sky
while startled wood ducks formation fly
and one woman dances as if alone.

*Taken from the Northern States Power company sign on the Red Cedar River hydroelectric dam in Menomonie.

Niagara, or Nothing, February 2017

—After Mary Oliver, "A Few Words," Blue Pastures

Driving to the hospital I want to tell you how
water cascades below West Clairemont bridge,
the Chippewa exploding in unexpected flood,
global warming like cancer springing, water's
feral fecundity, white caps goodbye kissing
gnarled roots and bent trunks along the shore.
"Life is Niagara, or nothing," Mary Oliver says,
the burgeoning rush of time meets the rocky
riverbanks full force. In a gray month when
nothing blooms but the scent of sap lifting,
beauty's bare arms still embrace the flood.

Haibun for Evergreen Cemetery in Winter

The snow-covered path reflects old bones, knotted tibia trunks and phalanges of oak, arbor vitae, and Norway Pine; trees, planted a century ago, show how seasons of sunlight suckled hope from Lake Menomin's breast, now a haven for ice shacks but still a place to ponder balance among the deer tracks, old stones, and circling crows, their harsh cries celebrating life.

shadows of crows
    wholly ghost evergreen
        sunlight speaking slant

Mad as a March Hare: March 2, 2017

> *Thanne þey begyn to swere
> and to stare, And be as
> braynles as a Marshe hare
> (Then they begin to swerve
> and to stare, And be as
> brainless as a March hare)*
> —Early English poem

Mad as a March hare,
I must take this road.
Neither lion nor lamb,
a woolly chimera day,
snow sweeps
the blacktop tongue.
Born from bitter
forget-me-not cold
and the bloodless
egg white maw
of Ash Wednesday's
snow slouched beast,
a toothy sunlit smile
hits ditched cars
along the asphalt breach.

your death
spontaneous generation
empty vases

The Romance of Dragonflies*

Four months after you pass
like a moth immolated
by incandescence,
I read the romance
of the blue morpho dragonfly,
bluest-of-skies Zenithoptera,
how his wings are living,
breathing layer cakes of light,
nanoscale spheres lying
between black blankets
of pigment reflecting
blue light through waxy
leaf-shaped crystals, and I think
how in your last sleep,
you still glowed,
the brilliant blue of bounty
slipping into final ultraviolet,
and I am not surprised to find
that despite world class color,
the morpho doesn't bother
with courtship display.
Life is too short:
Beauty alone is enough,
and when a female
flies near,
he grabs her.

*Susan Milius, "The Strangest Insect Wings," *Science News Magazine,* Vol. 191, No. 13, July 2017

Waltzing with Widow's Tears

    We   who
were soul mates in so   many ways could not
  learn   to waltz   together.
     That formal   fragile fitting
         of body   into body
      could not be mastered.
        Now I bend
         to waltz
           with
      Widow's Tears,
         named
           for
          their
       unplanned
        blooms,
          the
      irrevocable
       division
          of
         the
       leaves
       separ-
        ating
       flower
        from
       flower.

After You

Outside everywhere
alive with cicada song
leaffall longings

Corona of Women

August 21, 2017

Since you died,
I have walked in the company
of women. Unlike those haiku poets
who wondered river trails alone,
we walk together watching over one
who's forgotten her married name
but smiles with the light of decades,
women who happily pass
eclipse glasses back and forth
as we rest along the lake bank,
sharing darkness and the sliver
of bright light remaining
around the coronas
of our hearts.

The Great Unknowing

When you passed to the great unknowing,
your hospital bed was light house glass
I lost certainty to keep going.

In your last sleep, I saw you glowing;
I was lost in fog without compass,
hit by waves of my own unknowing.

My heart hands ached, but I kept rowing
around jagged rocks still locked in past;
I prayed for strength to keep on going.

Direction found in warm wind blowing,
I circled grief, a widening path,
the broken dock of my own unknowing.

Then a shore appeared where I could land.
As I shipped the oars, the fog unwrapped.
Unfolding the map of my unknowing,
I followed the light and kept going.

After Mary Oliver's "Wild Geese": Grieving Reconsidered*

Let go displacement, the harsh cries of
the goose lost from familiar flock. Seek
soft when hard scrabble paths obstruct your
animal life, and you limp doggedly thinking
of the flight two take together, lifting into lightness
your arms encircling ease from long practice. Em-
body now the strength those flights have given.
Love now what brightness is offered,
what sings of simple kindness in autumn night.
It will not be easy, but it will get easier.
Loves will come as grain left after harvest.

*The first words of each line form a line from "Wild Geese."

Twiggy

December, an old neighborhood, nine months
after you pass, and I want to tell you how
leaves on this tree dried but did not fall;
marcescence it's called, an attic's unread
manuscript, leaf spot blotting brown crumplings,
like spilled coffee on an earthy romance
someone had to write then could not discard.

An arborist blames too much rain this spring;
February, he says, all will be well,
but today this tree's no runway model,
baring her sylphlike, nearly naked self;
commodious instead, a squirrel nest,
nestled above speaks leafy confidence,
survival's old story, at least for now.

Negative Space

```
           The Japanese call it Ma.
     the empty space      between objects.
   It is the absence        that becomes central,
        At Tai Chi,       I fight the shape
         of an  invisible  opponent:
         the dissolution   of your warmth,
   the grief that rises    out of an Arctic infinite.
         Press of pain,         yield of air,
       We know each        other well now;
       the dance, not         dance goes on.
```

Winged Grief

When grief
has no shape but negative—
in the chair,   in the bed,
in the kitchen,   on the porch:
the vacuum of   the absent hug,
the body temperature
of outer space,
the shards of silence
breaking,
the only recourse
is to steal
some.

Tree Trimming

The
angel
at the top
never looks entirely
comfortable; maybe it's
her closeness to all those
Santas, Sugar Plum ballerinas.
rocking horses, teddy bears, and other
gaudy baubles of Christmas materialism.
I have tried to assuage her by adding more stars
and two herald angels, trumpets to mouths, but
she says that if she had her druthers everything would be
white and gold. I say, "Go back to your meditations.
Christmas is for everyone, the pagan as well as the ethereal—
even for one
whose only
gifts are empty
festooned packages of grief."
Eyes closed, she smiles: "Reread the *Tao,* in emptiness
there's potential."

February Flurry

Above
the treetops,
black birds exult gray sky.
No insects there, why joy?
Can crows drink snow on glide,
their tiny-boned tongues outstretched,
the air, the flakes, the dive,
flurries of intoxicants
tipplers drunk
on sky?

One Year, One Month

later I dream of you comfortable
in a corner of the Museum of Science
and Industry, the Ag Exhibition where
you hung out so often as a kid, now
providing a Peaceable Kingdom:
sunlight on fresh straw, new oak flooring,
round-eyed, gray and white kittens,
newly hatched, lemon yellow chicks,
and you stretched out, settling in
with your blessed, blissed, petting zoo grin,
letting the little ones come to you
as you always do, and I, standing
in the doorway, saying, "It looks like
you'll be here for a while; you know
I can't stay." You nod, and then we share
a gaze, decades made, deeply twined
by shared vision. Looking back once, I leave
through the upstairs of an old library,
past the card catalog of blessed places,
each step turned salt by unshed tears,
going home, unknowing where that is.

Walking with Turtles

To be away from home and yet to feel oneself everywhere at home; to see the world, to be at the centre of the world, and yet to remain hidden from the world—impartial natures which the tongue can but clumsily define.
   —Charles Baudelaire, "The Painter of Modern Life," New York: Da Capo Press, 1964. Orig. published in Le Figaro, 1863.

From the lodge steps, the lawn slants downward toward a line of Norway Pines, grass still wet with dew although it is nearly noon. Stepping mindfully across uneven ground, I coordinate breath with steps. Like the flamboyant French Flaneur, I walk with turtles, my shoes morphing; two painted turtles, Chrysemys picta, peregrinating practitioners of botanical study, ponderous, sole-searchers of the turf, nosing through rough cut blades of Kentucky Blue, crabgrass, clover and plaintain, nuzzling and snuffling, bodies massaged by tiny hands of grass. At St. Paul's Como Park Zoo, we once saw docents massaging Galapagos tortoises, two 500-pound master nappers, now awake, transported across oceans and continents by the pleasure of warm hands, a love shared that lifts them from their cool cement confines to be for those moments fully at home in the center of their world.

The Scent of Green

It is good to have an end to journey towards;
but it is the journey that matters, in the end.
—Ursula K. Le Guin, The Left Hand of Darkness

Green leaves smell green—
the profligate kindness of chlorophyll,
but beyond green there's more,
a subtle botanical bouquet,
its idiosyncratic chemical signature,
wafting and weaving olfactory paths:
maple leaf zap of sap,
rhubarb stem whiff of sour,
Tickweed's faint fragrance:
baby's bath soap;
briar patch where black cap nubs
change, faint green to tangerine:
subtle differences, scents of becoming;
late season dandelion leaf,
the peppery scent of success:
green grandmother energy,
focused on roots
now that her kids have gone.
Awash in scent songs,
a sun-spun bumble bee, big
as a thumb, *Flaneur** of foliage,
bumbles with purpose.

---

*A *Flaneur* is an elegant Parisian gentleman
who found personal purpose and pleasure
ambling through city neighborhoods.

Chasing Wild Grief

It cannot be lured with cups of fragrant wild orange tea
or trained with fluted bowls of chocolate mint ice cream.
Like the invisible ice stallion of the winter wind,
it cannot be saddled or broken by persistence.

Like the Windigo, it is huge and omnipresent,
sucking marrow from the bones of the day, and leaving
only strewn shards. The whinny of its woodwind
breath enters the inner ear, surrounds the heart,

starvation months stretching long, sinking down, down,
slipping past the tended topsoil of daily domestication,
past the bedrock of mythology into the plate
tectonics of the aching subterranean world.

Squirrel's Eye View

In the   cottonwood's   cleft
Squirrel posed between earth and sky,
almost   tree,
gray bark,   gray fur,   bright eye
poised   in   silent   meditation
the first   day   of   spring,
crocuses   emerging,
mourning   dove   on the   roof,
pale moon still visible half way up --
on the   Sea   of   Tranquility,
I see   your   sweet soul, awestruck
above   the   soft   dust.
In   my next life,   perhaps
I'll be a squirrel.

Junction Trail Revisited

Junction Trail Revisited

(after Ellen Kort "One by One"*)

Past the old rail
    Junction Trail,
the Red Cedar River
    runs like sweet cider
    down from the dam
where hydroelectric
    power first lit
city lights,
electrification,
    a celebration,
    an honoring,
    long awaited bright.
More than artifact,
    but no longer
    essential,
    the dam
still controls the flow:
when pressure builds,
    sluices open
    letting tension
    safely go,
a premeditative act
    like meditation.

When you were
    a river passing
wrapped in a gown
    of hospice sky blue,
    the sleep that passes
understanding,
    Fentanyl drip
floating through
    the last junction
    of a long conjunction
    the story I told and retold:
Walking to Musselburgh,
how we set forth
not knowing distance
    but warm in the sun,
    we walked together,
an easy path
between hedges
bright with blooms, and I
prayed through my telling
that you in your dreaming
would still know
I had not forsaken you.

Breathe in, breathe out,
slow, slow, slow,
*"the momentary kindness of letting go"

Darning
your / death,
the \ hole
in my / center,
those good   black   socks \ I wore so often that cold
March you lay dying, heathered wool, / white specks,   stars in the Milky Way,
above the smooth black darning egg,\ trilobite fossil I bought long ago,
Cambrian you said, palimpsest / of life, half a billion years old,
bright \ needle
first making a running stitch, rounding / honoring the edges, gently gathering
the hole smaller, then weaving back \ and forth across the emptiness,
shiny little   dips and flicks, / a Green Darner Dragonfly,
three
hundred
million
years old,
each
stitch
gently
covering
the
wound
in my
soul.

Walking in March
I found loose change in the street
and in budding trees

April 15

Glory be to spring for melting things,
for hearts that find sunlit spots to open—
In the parking lot of the Fresh Market,
a dragon of old snow expires slowly,
a toppling of stegs and crumpled wings,
dissolving into puddled black pavement,
bright rills slipping toward the drains.

You who did not believe in God,
but near-believed in dragons,
would have been sixty-nine today,
the numbers of your years yin-yang
like a late-sixties psychedelic poster,
melding light and dark, male and female,
as the dragon of marriage memories
folds tender wings around me.

Glissando for Wordsworth

—After Ted Kooser, "Étude"

I am looking at an earthworm uncovered
in s pile of mulched flowerbed leaves.
How it got there must have been intuitive,
as intimate an act as composing this poem—

cottonwood leaves decaying like memories,
how temporarily genderless, the poet reenacts
creation, slipping glissando through cool layers
until finding a place of rallentando repose,

luxuriating in the fugue of moist and dry
until timid light filtering through requiem
shockingly becomes a polytonality of blinding
bright, a glimpse of wideness so unexpected

that it must be abandoned accelerando
so that it might be reconsidered in reprise,
sliding into a secret soft pedal of earth,
disappearing beneath nodding daffodils.

For Michael: All Along Junction Trail

*Maybe any word rhymes with any other word,
more than any word rhymes with silence.*
—*William Stafford*

Monarchs rise like stained glass song.
We have walked this trail together.
What rhymes with the silence of your absence?
Bee balm slant rhymes pale pink to rose.

We have walked this trail together.
Red Admiral warms wings on wild rhubarb.
Bee balm slant rhymes lavender to rose.
White water dazzles, staying and leaving.

Red Admiral lifts wings on wild rhubarb,
Light glinting between sumac and poplar.
White water dazzles, leaving and staying.
Retaining wall crumbles in broken stone.

Light grinning from sumac to poplar,
A bench shimmers, overlooking the rapids,
Retaining wall stumbles in broken stone,
Osprey swoops past, clutching a shiner.

A bench silvers, overlooking the rapids,
Phoebe, "see me," up in box elder,
Osprey flaps past, clutching a shimmer,
Light dopplers on poplar leaves.

Phoebe, "feel me," bounces to basswood,
Words woven in nests of silence,
Talk dopplers through cottonwood leaves,
What rhymes with the silence of absence?

Words woven in nests of silence,
Weaving rye grass from summers' past tense,
What rhymes with the silence of absence?
Memories, rock at Red Cedar's edge,

Weaving dry grass for summers hence.
What rhymes with the silence of absence?
Memories rise from Red Cedar's edge.
Butterflies rock like stained glass song.

What rhymes with the silence of presence?
Butterflies rhyme like stained glass song.
We have walked this trail together.
You have been here all along.

South of the lake

A fox
lopes through
the old Catholic cemetery
fading flags and crumbling stones
bright tail banners
wild life

On Walking to Water:

The Campus 50 years later

From the footbridge,
the Chippewa River opens
like an ancient history textbook:

deep wisdom, unspent anger,
complex currents running beneath
a deceptively placid surface.

A small boat zigzags past,
life-vested men seeking the bodies
of two swimmers lost to impulse.

Amidst sunlit brilliance,
green-grass love and pheromones,
good colleges teach caution,

patience and planning—knowledge:
when and where to swim,
innocence paid quarterly.

Memories like mayflies
briefly skim the river's surface,
forever kissing goodbye.

Mind Music

All the choir of heaven and furniture of earth—
in a word, all those bodies which compose the frame of the world—
have not any subsistence without a mind.
—George Berkeley

On a beautiful spring day
it is possible to see the angel choir
holding up the heavens.
Resplendent
in their infinite blue gowns
and fluffy white wings,
the sopranos and altos float
barefoot slightly above the grass,
creating an upward momentum—
daffodils, lilacs, babies in prams,
ultrasonic opening melodies
defining earth's potential for upness,
while the baritones and basses
buttressing the bedrock
through their Birkenstock sandals,
do heavy lifting in the rear,
the vault of the cosmos balanced
on their infrasonic harmonies,
and when the clefs of blooming
and booming intertwine in a frame
of exquisite choral connection,
the carousels of earth all turn.

In late September I plant Dutch Iris bulbs,

1.
an optimism of onion domes,
an inherent potential
for gold and cerulean,
early summer sun and sky.

Small bulbs lie firm in my hand,
consecutive candles,
each holding a cache of light,
copywritten resurrection.

I measure with my eyes
spaces where each set goes.
On a day of intermittent rain,
A rooster crows and crows—

2.
But moment begs mythology;
random threads woven in
tapestry always tell truth and lie;
reality ravels with messy edges,

and animal hunger has a way
of eating human intention.
The next morning, I found
only empty indentations,

and the fat gray scoundrel,
perched wary in my maple,
digesting the colors of summer,
intimations of life eternal.

March, Cirque du Soul

The gray squirrel that died
on the lawn last night was light,
possibly starved, forgetting its cache
of black walnuts buried below snow.
Although considering what I found
planting daffodils last October
included a golf ball and a silver
marble, perhaps it wasn't sensible,
preferring the novel over the edible.

The gray squirrel that died
on the lawn last night was light,
its rigored legs splayed like
a disk that could sail if thrown,
but bright had gone from its eyes
and pink, faded from its nose
when I lifted it with my shovel
and buried it beneath the pine,
its art of ascendance lost,
an elegy to winter's cost.

Tundra Swans

The tundra swans I saw flying are gone;
they flew northward above Lake Menomin
toward the Red Cedar, the headwaters
of the Chippewa and then Lake Superior,
Gitchi Manitou, Great Creator,
winging the western shore to Canada,
and their summer nesting grounds.

These were whistlers, *c. columbianus;*
although above my purring engine,
I heard nothing. But soul struck by a flash
of stunning white plumage and six-foot spans,
it was as if I flew with them, a honey
moon trip as we once took, that exuberant
pump of wings and upward soar above
dappled shallows where wild rice once grew,
as if anything were more important,
and I knew that moment there was not.

Discovery

The night of our anniversary,
you three years stardust,
deer ate the lilies.
The glowing Stargazer
we chose together
had just opened, its sunstruck
petals too perfect to be real,
now haute cuisine
for white-tailed ungulates
drawn to its stellar bouquet.
I wanted to shoot them,
my pacifism momentarily
overcome in the gravity
of an exploding star.

October, Junction Trail Redux

A gentle rain, gently fades,
sumac scarlet, the Red Cedar
running fast, down
from the Tainter Gates
in the dam, rapids, ripples,
sparkle, pressure relief,
exhaled breath of the wild.

In the years since you died
I have watched a pair
of sneakers thrown high
into the arching boughs
of a maple, a moldering
dance that remains, fading
into the shadows, ghost
shoes, high stepping the air.

About the Author

Sandra J. Lindow has had a lifelong devotion to poetry. Her first published poem appeared in a Sunday School magazine when she was eleven. Her poetry collections include: *Rooted in the Earth* (1989), *The Heroic Housewife Papers* (1990), *A Celebration of Bones* (1996), *Revision Quest* (1997), *Walking the Labyrinth* (2004), *Touched by the Gods* (2008), *The Hedge Witch's Upgrade* (2012), and *Amazonned: A Woman Warriors Guide to Breast Cancer and Recovery* (2019).

In 1990, *Heroic Housewife* won the Council for Wisconsin Writers' Posner Award for the best poetry collection by a Wisconsin writer. Her poem "If Death: A Pre-Primer" was included in *The Year's Best Fantasy and Horror: 2001*. In 2003, she received the Wisconsin Press Women's Award for Poetry. In 2003 and 2018, she won first prize awards in the Wisconsin Fellowship of Poets' Triad Contest, and in 2020 she received their Muse Prize for poetry. In 2004 and 2011, she received Jade Ring first prize awards in poetry from the Wisconsin Writers' Association. In 2018, she accepted the Blei Award for Poetry.

Her poetry has appeared in markets such as *The Dwarf Stars Anthologies, The Rhysling Anthologies, Star*Line, Asimov's, Scifaikuest, Dreams and Nightmares, Tales of the Talisman,* and *The Magazine of Speculative Poetry*. Her work can be found online in *Verse Wisconsin* archives, *Word Gathering, Blue Heron Review, Strange Horizons, Eye to the Telescope, UpNorth Lit,* and *Sky Island*.

Since 1987, she has served as West Central Vice President of the Wisconsin Fellowship of Poets. Since retiring, she continues to do freelance writing, reviewing, and editing. She lives on a hilltop in Menomonie, Wisconsin. Her husband, Michael Levy, died on April 4, 2017. More can be found at https://www.wfop.org/member-pages#/sandra-lindow.

www.ingramcontent.com/pod-product-compliance
Lightning Source LLC
Chambersburg PA
CBHW021026090426
42738CB00007B/921